P9-DHE-693

THE PUMPKIN BOOK

BY GAIL GIBBONS

HOLIDAY HOUSE · NEW YORK

FOR JOHN MORALE

Copyright © 1999 by Gail Gibbons
All rights reserved
Printed in the United States of America
First Edition

Library of Congress Cataloging-in-Publication Data
Gibbons, Gail.
　　The pumpkin book / by Gail Gibbons. — 1st ed.
　　　　p.　　cm.
　　Summary: Describes how pumpkins come in different shapes and
sizes, how they grow, and their traditional uses and cultural
significance. Includes instructions for carving a pumpkin and drying
the seeds.
　　ISBN 0-8234-1465-5
　　1. Pumpkin—Juvenile literature.　[1. Pumpkin.]　I. Title.
SB347.G535　1999　98-45267　CIP　AC
635'.62—dc21

Special thanks to Bob Welch
of Shearer's Greenhouses,
Bradford, Vermont

Pumpkins come in all shapes and sizes.

DILL'S
ATLANTIC GIANT

JACK BE LITTLE

BABY BEAR

CONNECTICUT
FIELD

LUMIN

Pumpkins are members of the squash family. There are
many different kinds of pumpkins. Small pumpkins. Big
pumpkins. Round pumpkins. Tall pumpkins.

RED OCTOBER

BIG MAX

SMALL
SUGAR
PIE

TRICK OR
TREAT

Gardeners and farmers call them pumpkin varieties. Some pumpkins have a smooth skin and others have lots of bumps.

In the springtime, when the sun's rays begin to warm the soil, it is planting time. Some gardeners turn the soil to get it ready to plant a small pumpkin patch. A pumpkin patch is where pumpkins are grown.

Some farmers use their plows to slice through and turn over the dirt. The field will eventually be a huge pumpkin patch.

PUMPKIN SEED

BEGINNING OF A PUMPKIN

FOOD

SEED COAT

PUMPKIN SEEDS

The soil is ready. It is time to plant the pumpkin seeds. The beginning of a pumpkin is curled up inside each pumpkin seed. Food is stored there, too. The seed has a seed coat on the outside to protect it. The bigger the seed, the bigger the variety of pumpkin that will grow.

Sometimes pumpkin seeds are planted in rows. Other times they are planted in small circular areas called hills. Several shallow holes are poked into the hill and one pumpkin seed is dropped into each hole and covered with dirt. Each hill should be about 3 feet (1m) to 6 feet (2m) apart to give the plants lots of room to grow.

A pumpkin seed won't sprout until the dirt is warm and water has soaked the seed to soften its coat. Once the seed coat breaks open, a root begins to grow down into the soil. It takes in water and minerals from the soil for food.

SEED LEAVES

After about one week, two leaves appear where each pumpkin seed was planted. These smooth leaves are called seed leaves. They begin to make more food for the plant from the sunlight and air.

PUMPKIN VINE LEAVES

VINE

After a few days, small pumpkin vine leaves appear. These leaves look different. They are prickly and have rough, jagged edges. More new vine leaves grow. Stems begin to grow and twist, crawling along the ground as they become vines.

FLOWER

TENDRILS

The vines grow thicker and thicker. They grow curly tendrils that wrap themselves around other parts of the plant to help spread the vines. Gold-colored flowers begin to bloom.

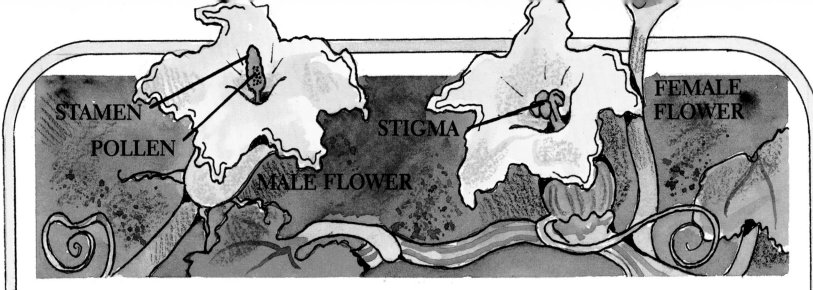

STAMEN
POLLEN
MALE FLOWER
STIGMA
FEMALE FLOWER

NECTAR is the sweet juice flowers make.

A pumpkin begins to grow when a grain of pollen from the stamen of a male pumpkin flower lands on the stigma of a female pumpkin flower. This is called pollination. Sometimes pollen moves from flower to flower when the wind blows. Bees and other insects help pollinate, too. Pollen rubs on and off their bodies as they travel from flower to flower in search of nectar.

SMALL PUMPKIN

The female flower has a small green ball beneath its blossom. When the flower is pollinated, the little ball begins to grow. It is a very, very small pumpkin. Over time it becomes bigger…

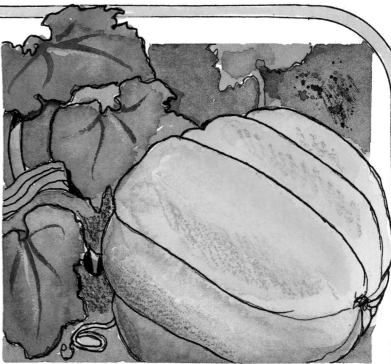

and bigger . . . and bigger. The pumpkin's skin begins to turn from green to orange. All of the pumpkins in the pumpkin patch begin to turn orange.

In the fall, when the vines begin to dry up and die, it is harvest time. It usually takes from 80 to 120 days, depending on the variety, for a seed to grow into a ripened pumpkin. It is ready to pick if it feels hard on the outside and sounds hollow when it is tapped.

Often shears are used to clip the pumpkins from their vines, leaving about 3 inches (7.5cm) of stem. The stem helps to keep the harvested pumpkin from getting moldy.

During the fall, more and more pumpkins of many shapes and sizes appear at roadside stands and in stores.

Fall makes people think of country fairs. Sometimes awards are given for the biggest, the prettiest or the strangest pumpkin grown.

The biggest pumpkin ever grown was in New York State in 1996. It weighed about as much as a small car . . . 1,061 pounds (481kg)! At fairs there are pumpkin pie tasting contests, too.

When the Pilgrims came to the New World, friendly Native American Indians showed them how to plant pumpkins. Often, the Indian women were the pumpkin farmers of their tribes. The Pilgrims ate pumpkins every day in different forms such as pumpkin bread, pumpkin pie and pumpkin seed cereal.

Thanksgiving reminds people of the Pilgrims' first harvest season. They wanted to give thanks for the food they would have through the cold winter months. They celebrated by having a Thanksgiving feast.

Halloween is on October 31st. A long time ago people believed that ghosts, witches and goblins roamed around that night. Some people built bonfires to scare them away.

Later, October 31st was called All Hallows Even, which means holy evening. It was the night before a church festival called All Hallows or All Saints Day. All Hallows Even was shortened to Halloween. Today, Halloween is celebrated in different ways.

HOW TO CARVE A PUMPKIN

1. ALWAYS have an adult help you.

2. Take a knife that is not too sharp or a special cutter used for carving pumpkins and cut the lid off the pumpkin.

3. Take a big spoon and scoop out the seeds and insides of the pumpkin. You can save the seeds to dry and eat later, or to plant for next year's pumpkins.

4. Draw the design you want using a pencil or a washable magic marker.

5. Cut along the lines you drew. Be careful and ALWAYS carve away from yourself.

6. Wipe away any magic marker lines and put the lid back on your pumpkin. It's ready for Halloween!

There are pumpkins! It's great fun to carve pumpkins into what you want them to be. Funny pumpkins. Scary pumpkins. Beautifully carved pumpkins.

ALWAYS have an adult place and light the candle.

Some people place a candle or a light inside and light it so the pumpkin will shine in all its glory on Halloween night.

Other people decorate pumpkins with paint, glitter and other decorations. These pumpkins can last a long time because they haven't been carved.

No two pumpkins are alike. They all have their very own personalities.

All lined up on Halloween night they are a glowing sight to behold.

Isn't it amazing that all this began with a few small pump-kin seeds? Glow pumpkins, glow!

PUMPKINS . . .

Pumpkins probably originated in North America. Pumpkin seeds that are 9000 years old have been found in caves in Mexico.

Native American Indians often planted pumpkins with corn and beans. The Iroquois Indians believed corn, beans and pumpkins were a gift from their Sun God. These three crops are called the Three Sisters.

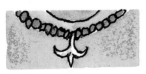

The Pueblo Indians of the Southwest often design pumpkin blossoms into their silver jewelry.

The word pumpkin comes from the French word "pompion," which means ripened by the sun.

Sometimes the Pilgrims dried pumpkin shells to use as bowls.

Sometimes carved pumpkins are called jack-o'-lanterns. The word jack-o'-lantern comes from an old fable about a mean and stingy man named Jack. When he died it was rumored that he was forced to roam around the world carrying a turnip with a hot, glowing coal inside. People called him Jack of the Lantern or Jack-o'-lantern.

Pumpkins are full of vitamin A, which can help give one strong teeth, good vision and smooth skin.

Few pumpkin flowers actually do become pumpkins. This is because the female blossom opens for pollination for only one day in its entire life.

Everyone loves pumpkin pie, especially around Thanksgiving. Some people like to eat dried pumpkin seeds, too.

HOW TO DRY YOUR PUMPKIN SEEDS

1. Separate the seeds from the pumpkin pulp and rinse under cold water.

2. Spread the seeds in a thin layer on a screen, cookie sheet or big dish to air-dry, preferably in direct sunlight, for several days.

3. Once the seeds are completely dry, put them in a jar with a tight lid for storage. You can eat them or plant them next year to grow more pumpkins.

PUMPKIN